Chiseled by Choices

Chiseled by Choices

Reflections on Empowerment, Growth and Healing

LIFE CHANGE SERIES

VOLUME 2

Lady D

INGLEWOOD, CALIFORNIA

Paperback ISBN: 979-8-9871789-4-2
eBook ISBN: 979-8-9871789-5-9
Cover design and interior formatting by Open Heart Designs

Extending a virtual hug to the souls traveling with me…

To my mom, for the gift of life.

To my son and daughter—for being the wind beneath my wings.

To my grandson and granddaughter—for being the crown jewels that light up my life.

To my Angels, Nikita Jackson and Rochelle Eubanks—for sharing your heart with everyone drawn to this work.

To my reader—
Thank you for choosing this moment, this work, and this reflective journey. May you find the courage to reflect on what gives your life meaning and purpose as you move through the text. Your insights will pay dividends across a lifetime.

Contents 

Special Message From The Author

The *Life Change Series* by *Flyte Time Publications* shares authentic stories to elevate readers to new heights one book at a time.

I decided to publish this volume after reading the *Wellness in 8 Dimensions Guide: Exploring Strengths and Building New Wellness Habits* by Peggy Swarbrick.[1] This 14-page guide challenged me to examine the unfolding of my coming-of-age story through a definition of wellness I never considered before. Something I immediately thought might be helpful to others seeking to connect the dots of their lived experience.

The definition of wellness that opened my eyes to see that there's more to all of us than meets the eye states:

"Wellness is not the absence of disease, illness, and stress but the presence of:

— purpose in life
— active involvement in satisfying work and play
— joyful relationships
— a healthy body and living environment
— happiness."

This definition captures the essence of the eight dimensions of wellness that work in tandem to help us live a life of significance. This holistic view of wellness offers an opportunity to gain a deeper understanding of what we need to experience empowerment, growth, and healing throughout our lives. Figure 1, *Tree of Wellness*, offers a visual representation of the eight intersecting dimensions.

I've paraphrased the definition of each dimension, which I will refer to as *facets* throughout the book to align with my view that each of us is a *diamond in the rough.*

- **Emotional wellness** means recognizing, naming, and responding to our feelings with honesty and care.
- **Environmental wellness** refers to the spaces we live in and move through, and how these environments can affect our peace, energy, and safety.
- **Financial wellness** is about building a relationship with money that reduces stress and supports our freedom and dignity.
- **Intellectual wellness** is about staying curious, learning, and thinking in ways that keep our minds growing.
- **Occupational wellness** includes finding meaning in how we spend our time—through work, caregiving, or creative endeavors.
- **Physical wellness** involves caring for the body—through rest, nourishment, movement, and regular attention.
- **Social wellness** is cultivated through meaningful relationships that support our sense of connection and belonging.
- **Spiritual wellness** involves drawing strength from our faith, life purpose, or a deeper sense of meaning. (See Figure 1)

Each of these facets requires our tender loving care from the cradle to the grave. But with so many moving parts, it can be challenging to honor and acknowledge how well we're doing in each area. Therein lies the rub and the opportunity to make better choices.

As a diamond in the rough, we can celebrate our wins and at the same time make a conscious decision to resolve our inner struggles and overcome external barriers that shade our shine. Meaning, we can stop, look, and listen to what our soul is saying anytime.

But how many times do the facets of wellness that remain a work in progress, in need of shining, end up dictating our choices, sometimes for our good, and sometimes to our detriment?

As you engage with the stories in this book which shed light on this question, I hope you embrace the opportunity to examine the unfolding of your life through the prism of the eight facets of wellness interwoven in the text. At the end of each chapter, you'll find blank pages to use however you like.

Figure 1

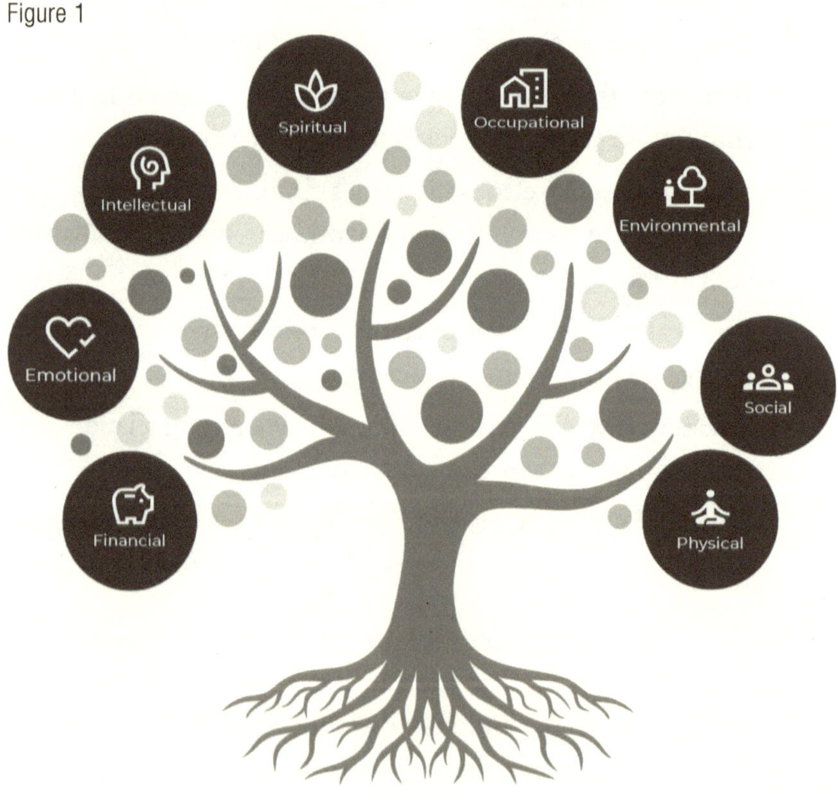

Introduction

Chiseled by Choices: Reflections on Empowerment, Growth, and Healing is more than a self-help book; it's an invitation to engage in the most important work of your life. It's for the soul ready to embark on a journey of *empowerment, growth, and healing* by recognizing that our daily decisions shape the outcomes of our ever-unfolding coming-of-age story.

Empowerment is about recognizing our strengths, using our voice, and making choices that align with who we are and who we are becoming. *Growth* is about learning from our experiences, stretching beyond our comfort zone, and allowing new opportunities to enlarge our vision of what's possible. *Healing* is about bringing our mind, body, and spirit into alignment with our gifts and talents so we can step into our divine purpose and calling, whatever that might be.

These creative gifts of the spirit—*empowerment, growth, and healing*—are the foundation for living a life of significance. The longer I live, the more I realize the things that weigh us down are equal-opportunity employers. But I've discovered there are things we can lean into, like hurdlers, to overcome obstacles that hinder wholehearted living, the key to living our best life.

Divided into three parts, Volume II of the Life Change Series presents authentic stories rooted in lived experience to delve into matters of the heart that can mold, shape, and influence us for a time, a season, or a lifetime.

Part I — Soul Talking

Delves into the importance of acknowledging and processing whatever causes us to experience pain, grief, and loss — all of which may become a catalyst for profound growth and the restoration of our ability to make life-affirming choices.

Part II — The Quiet Work That Heals

Explores the unseen work of transformation to affirm that no matter how our lives begin, we are not powerless to change. We have everything we need to bring about the change we seek — *courage, curiosity, and imagination.*

Part III — The Power of Wholehearted Living

Shares empowering perspectives, creative insights, and practical tools for fulfilling our potential by living a life that aligns with our hopes, dreams, and aspirations.

The Epilogue connects the dots by elevating the importance of our divine purpose and calling to its rightful place, where nothing about our lived experience is wasted. When we reach this stage of life, our essence and brilliance shines bright, reflecting what it means to be "Chiseled by Choices."

— PART I —

Soul Talking

Uncovering the essence of who we are begins with a conversation — at the top of the list is the conversation we are willing to have with ourselves.

Soul talking is the honest dialogue that arises with — questions, confessions, and realizations that stir us. It's where our innermost innermost being speaks, where memory testifies, and the truth of our lived experience begins to rise.

But for each of us, the conversation will begin with whatever we're dealing with — loss, forgiveness, a new beginning, or the stillness that comes with change and transition. Soul talking can surface in many ways. It invites us to listen, to name our truth, and to make peace with what we find.

CHAPTER 1

The Transformative Power of Pain

> *"When we deny the full expression of our grief, it lays like a weight on our hearts, causing emotional pain and physical ailments."*
>
> — bell hooks

WHILE DRAFTING THE MANUSCRIPT FOR this volume, my mom died. The text message received at 4:39 a.m. said, "*She's gone, Auntie.*" The official time of death, 3:39 a.m., Pacific Time—three days shy of my mom's eighty-fourth birthday. Upon rising, I sent a love note of remembrance in prayer to my mom for bringing me into the world.

After reading the message a second time, an eerie sense of relief descended upon me. I'd been waiting to exhale all my life. There's something about the mother-child connection that takes your breath away, a little each day, when the ride-or-die connection you dreamed of never arrives. So when I exhaled, it was the final act of a chapter decades in the making.

Unbeknownst to anyone but me, when my mom took her last breath, she set me free from pursuing an *umbilical love* that never manifested in my life. The long-awaited exhale relieved the weight of a fractured relationship that was never mine to fix.

Even though the levees of my soul broke, the emotions suppressed over the years were too painful to sit with. *I didn't break down and cry, lose my mind, or ask God why?* My mom, a rolling stone, had finally come to rest in a place that deprived me of the opportunity to reconcile with her on this side of heaven.

Believe me when I say, "There are no words to convey what it feels like to miss out on the opportunity to become someone's daughter." But grief, like a waterfall, pierced the landscape of my heart and shaped the contours of my memory for six decades. The day of my mom's passing placed a demand on my soul to mourn something I never had, to sit with the emptiness that shaped my existence, and allow the transformative power of pain to do its thing.

Truncated and *complicated* are the words my soul gravitates to when grappling with the relationship with my mom. Across six decades, we lived under the same roof for twenty-two months, our relationship never had a chance to bloom.

At eleven months old, I was removed from her care for reasons that remain a mystery—poverty, abuse, neglect? I'll never know. But the severance of our ties set the stage for navigating life as a *motherless child.* A situation that did not make my heart grow fonder. It disturbed and disrupted the unity of mind, body, and spirit I needed to feel comfortable in my own skin.

Over the course of fifteen years, I lived in three foster homes, which impacted me in ways my soul knows all too well:

- I struggled to form a sense of identity and self-worth.
- I wrestled with vulnerability, transparency, and trust.
- I sought safety in perfectionism, performance, and people-pleasing.

- I sunk into patterns of invisibility to avoid being outed as a foster child, and
- I never bet on myself.

I ended up questioning my worth in ways I couldn't even name, moving through life with uncertainty about where I belonged. Nobody knew the trouble I'd seen but Jesus.

During my last pit stop at a group home for girls, I tried to make sense of my predicament by diving into self-help books. One weekend—I curled up with *Necessary Losses: The Loves, Illusions, Dependencies, and Impossible Expectations That All of Us Have to Give Up in Order to Grow*. I devoured the book which offered clues for processing what was weighing me down—the loss of umbilical love.

The book offered more than clues—it helped me acknowledge a few things:

- Loss is a part of growth.
- Our early attachments and bonds, or the lack thereof, shape how we think, feel, and behave.
- Perfection is not the standard for gauging how well mothers manage their divine assignment.
- Separation is inevitable at some point in life, and
- Acknowledging grief creates space for healing.

Years later, I discovered Brené Brown, whose words mirrored the theme of Necessary Losses. In *Rising Strong—The Reckoning, The Rumble, The Revolution*, she said:

> *"We must never forget we are the authors of our own lives. We write our own daring endings. We craft love from heartbreak, compassion from shame, grace from disappointment, courage from failure. Showing up is our power."*

When I entered the twilight of my young adult years, I had to face the fact that *showing up* was easier said than done. The loss of a mother's love at any age, for whatever reason, is tough. It's a major life event, a turning point, a hard stop that impacts our emotional, physical, social, and spiritual facets of wellness—and how we show up. But showing up is our power, our birthright, a sacred energy that no one can diminish without our permission.

Throughout the years, I never gave anyone permission, not even my absentee mom, to dictate how I showed up. I never received a mental health diagnosis of any kind, but I knew something was amiss. You know something's wrong when, more often than not, you feel empty, numb, hopeless, and withdrawn.

On the inside, I was dying of starvation from the lack of maternal love. I still remember the day my soul bookmarked the moment the pains of life crept in—to short-circuit my ability to tap into courage, curiosity, and imagination. These were gifts of the spirit that I needed to show up better. The lack of access to what empowered me to pivot and shift during times of distress, negatively impacted the emotional, physical, social, and spiritual facets of my health and wellness.

The disconnect led to the onset of *desolation*, a heart posture and spiritual condition described by Margaret Silf, author of *Inner Compass*, as a state of being withdrawn, isolated, drained, and cut off from yourself and others. Desolation put a name on what it looked like to show up under the influence of several rounds of separation, severance, and loss. It also exposed the hidden cost of living with unresolved grief, which lays like a weight on your heart, causing intense emotional pain.

As a motherless child, I wrestled with the pains of life. Yet by the grace of God, I escaped the haunting embrace and mind-numbing grip of suicidal ideation on three occasions. The escape route extended by grace became larger when I discovered the healing power of creative expression through music.

I fell in love with the artistry of Patti LaBelle, the "Godmother of Soul." By singing and dancing to her songs, which carried more than a melody, I eased the discomfort of family separation, the sting of invisibility, and fear of the unknown. Song and dance became a way to replace the pains of life shading my shine with the liberating balm of self-expression. "Music Is My Way of Life" by Patti La Belle wasn't just a song—it was a *lifeline* that lifted my spirit and stirred something deep inside of me: the will to live.

Music unlocked portals of understanding that formal education could never reveal by giving voice to feelings inside of me that longed to be set free. There were times when the tempo of a melody released the suppressed parts of me. Whether it came through love ballads, the grit of rhythm and blues, the sway of reggae, or the uplifting sounds of gospel, music led me to believe I could do anything with the right playlist.

Stand, by Sly and the Family Stone, emboldened me to throw down the gauntlet and stop trying to meet other people's expectations. Even on my worst day, I found joy in listening to *Don't Worry, Be Happy* by Bobby McFerrin, while *Exodus* by Bob Marley and the Wailers set the stage for branding myself as a woman on the rise.

The more I turned to music, the more I awakened to the redemptive and resurrecting power of creative expression. *Home* by Stephanie Mills beckoned me and my inner child to stop running wild, to bloom where planted, and learn to be at home with ourselves during periods of desolation and times of distress. *Optimistic* by Sounds of Blackness gave me permission to dance through seasons of uncertainty with hope in the dawn of a new day. Far beyond entertainment, music became a lifeline for linking up with joy.

By allowing my soul to lead the way, I stumbled onto something that revived the suppressed parts of me. Music and dance as alternative pathways to healing,[2] empowered me to process my pain, reclaim my voice, and lighten the load of what was weighing me down.

In the days following my mother's passing, I found myself—leaning into the healing power of music to face another day in my coming-of-age-story. This time, I immersed myself in the vision projected by the lyrics of *"We Gon' Be Alright"* by Tye Tribbett.

My mother's passing represented a rite of passage everyone must contend with—the inevitability of life and death. It also became an opportune time to pay homage to these words: "You may not control all the events that happen to you, but you can decide not to be reduced by them."—Maya Angelou

More than anything, my mother's passing presented an unexpected opportunity to surrender to something I resisted for decades—the transformative power of pain. Even though I didn't get to be the daughter I dreamed of, I'm grateful for the lessons learned along the way, the most memorable being, *"Love is the most durable power in the world."*—Dr. Martin Luther King Jr.

Throughout the years, I found courage in these words to endure coming-of-age in a melting pot of adversity. They also provided strength for navigating the unending waves of maternal grief and loss across six decades. The kind of love envisioned by Dr. King is *agape love*, which is demonstrated by a heart willing to create space for the *truncated* and *complicated* people in our lives. Agape love is unconditional, sacrificial, and not always reciprocated. Yet strong enough to embrace those who stir mixed emotions within us.

Several weeks after my mom's passing, I attended her homegoing service—a small, solemn, and surreal affair attended by two of her nine children. The most painful part involved listening to reflections about how much she loved and cared for others—which did not resonate with me but disturbed and shook me to the core. I attempted to leave mid-service when tears began to flow from the sinkhole in my soul, but, with my daughter holding one hand and my niece the other, I remained seated.

In spite of the discomfort, the service created space for the transformative power of pain to have her perfect work in my life. A work that removed the weighted veil of regret from my heart. Freeing me to live from the inside out, no longer bound by the emotional turbulence of my infant, adolescent, teen, and young adult years.

The release from regret—made me feel like a bird taking flight. For a moment I ascended into the precious memories related to my time in vitro—the good times we managed to share for 22 months—and the inviting, yet distant warmth of my mother's million-dollar smile. These fleeting and precious memories will always live in the crypt of my lived experience.

Pain can be overwhelming, but it can also usher in long-awaited healing if we're willing to sit with it, as I did.

Even when it enters uninvited, pain carries the potential to awaken, mold, and shape us. Pain can open a door to wholehearted living by creating space for the emergence of deeper levels of introspection and authenticity:

- *Pain as a Mirror* can urge us to confront truths we'd rather not face.
- *Pain as a Teacher* can help us understand why boundaries and empathy matter.
- *Pain as a Purifier* can help us strip away false narratives and unrealistic expectations.
- *Pain as a Compass* can guide us toward our divine purpose and calling.
- *Pain as a Spark* can ignite us to embrace disappointment as an opportunity for growth.
- *Pain as a Reset Button* can help us reboot when we miss the mark.

— *Pain as a Creative Source* can inspire us to share our gifts and talents with the world.

Pain is so much more than something to endure. It can set us free to explore and unveil the facets of our health and wellness temporarily overshadowed by setbacks, challenges, and disruptive life events.

Notes

CHAPTER 2

The Wisdom of Lived Experience

"I am not what happened to me. I am what I choose to become."

— CARL JUNG

NO MATTER HOW MANY TIMES I circle the sun—my lived experience with emotional and generational trauma is here to stay. It's impossible for me to unsee what I've seen, undo what I've felt, erase what I've endured, and disregard what I've overcome.

While circling the sun, the speed at which life unfolds rarely presents an opportunity to engage in a *purposeful pause* to consider how our backstory has shaped our journey. Maya Angelou said, "There is no greater agony than bearing an untold story inside of you," [3] and I agree.

The retelling of what the soul already knows can become a source of empowerment, growth, and healing. The reflections in this chapter delve into the healing power of truth-telling to reveal how the wisdom of our lived experience can arise to illuminate a path forward.

As a guiding light, wisdom is something we all possess. It's not reserved for the elite, aged, rich and famous, or influencers. Wisdom rises to the surface when our lived experience and times of reflection meet to engage in soul-talking to amplify the beauty and uniqueness of our life journey.

The wisdom that guides my choices and decisions grew out of the backstory of what I lived through. The melting pot of adversity I stewed in until aging out of care could have burned me to a crisp. But it didn't. I emerged a little dinged up, but solid as a rock—a diamond in the rough. The flames of instability and sting of family separation strengthened my resolve to master the possibility of change during seasons of adversity.

The days of living among peers in care taught me things I could never have learned otherwise:

- How to walk and talk with people who didn't look like me.
- How to be at home with myself on any given day.
- How to make do with the unpredictable love of caregivers.
- How to show up with a forgiving heart.
- How to trust the intuition arising from within.

The greatest lesson learned over the years was how to pivot and shift without breaking when the prospect of reuniting with family remained a moving target.

If someone were to ask, "What kept you across the decades of separation from your mom?" I'd share two things: living among peers who believed we were more than what happened to us and opening my heart to the wisdom of the Bible. These things created a framework for keeping my eye on what mattered most—and living in alignment with it.

- Being a person who kept their word
- Treating others the way I wanted to be treated

- Being a receiver and extender of grace rather than a recycler of hate, and
- Leaving Others Viable and Edified (LOVE) at all times

Extending love to others never presented a problem for me, but I struggled with self-love and self-acceptance.

Without oversharing, this is how my lived experience with personal and generational trauma manifested in my life. As outgoing, congenial, and compassionate as I appeared to be, I was not totally free. I remained immobilized in matters of the heart after experiencing harmful sexual events during my younger years.

The lingering effects made it difficult to trust and cultivate meaningful relationships as a young adult. My body reacted by remaining on high alert—constantly scanning my surroundings for safety and security threats, among foster family siblings, frenemies, co-workers, and potential suitors.

I entered my thirties as an embattled queen fighting demons only I could see. The twists and turns on my insecurities had me living a double life. One day I found myself basking in the overflow of hope and all that it entailed, then I'd lapse without a cause into playing small for weeks. Some days I moved with confidence, and on others I hid behind self-doubt. There were times when I really wanted to connect with someone but found myself pulling back due to the fear of rejection.

Vulnerability and transparency were never my thing. Even though I succeeded in projecting the image of a strong woman who had it all together, my heart told a different story. Beneath the layers of self-protection lay a soul in search of empowerment, growth, and healing rather than pretense. But somewhere along the way, I started editing my truth by withholding the expression of my needs, wants, and desires. I didn't want people to brand me as demanding or needy.

My struggle with self-love and self-acceptance was real. It created a wall of resistance and barrier that kept me from getting close to people, which at some point would require disclosing the gaping holes in my family tree. I was afraid that sharing my truth would drive people away. So I spent the better part of my young adult years stage managing, orchestrating, and rationing the flow of genuine love and affection towards the people in my life.

For reasons that did not set right with me, my life was unfolding in ways that mirrored sentiments expressed by Marianne Williamson, author of "Our Deepest Fear":

> Our deepest fear is not that we are inadequate.
>
> Our deepest fear is that we are powerful beyond measure.
>
> It is our light, not our darkness, that most frightens us. [4]

These sentiments prompted me to consider if my self-protective and controlling habits were rooted in something that didn't begin with me—generational trauma. Generational trauma consists of unconscious habits and repeated cycles of behavior which can seep into our lives through the family bloodline.

With the enthusiasm and excitement of a game show contestant, I wanted to know:

— Was I reenacting patterns of behavior passed down by my mother?

— Was I mirroring what I experienced vicariously during the freefall from my mother's care—her detached, guarded, and withdrawn spirit?

— Was I allowing emotional triggers linked to the disruptive and harmful events I experienced to dictate my choices and decisions when it came to matters of the heart?

These questions led me to engage in a *purposeful pause* to consider what might be buried beneath the surface of my lived experience. My time of reflection revealed that the removal from my mother's care unraveled the very best part of me, a loving and trusting heart. This shook me to the core because it exposed the true source of my self-protective habits. I also discovered that the link between family separation at an early age and the way I handled matters of the heart remained a sore spot.

For reasons that did not begin with me, love became something I managed rather than experienced. My trio of bad habits, rationing love and affection, suppressing emotions for fear of losing control, and coming off as a bad bitch, didn't begin with me. They were nothing more than a reenactment of sorts of the hallmark of my mother's behavior.

The return of what I thought I'd lost—a loving and trusting heart—began as the wisdom of my lived experience kicked in to reveal:

- What happened to me was not my fault.
- I didn't do anything to bring about the severance of my family tree.
- I didn't consent to the abuse experienced in care.

These disclosures led me to believe I could change the unfolding of my coming-of-age story by embracing *the power of choice*, *agency*, and *free will.*

The power of choice prompted me to distance myself from coping mechanisms that were not a good fit. Agency invited me to lean into choices that aligned with my values. Free will encouraged me to break free from self-limiting beliefs by declaring: "I am not what happened to me. I am what I choose to become."

Facing off with so many things at once left me searching for strength to distance myself from what I discovered. As a woman who had her light dimmed by painful life events, I decided to connect to a power source far greater than me—the Creator of heaven and earth, to help me resist the temptation of self-protective habits—triggered by trauma. The Bible assured me that nothing could separate me from the redemptive love of the One who knew me before He placed me in my mother's womb, Romans 8:38–39 and Jeremiah 1:5 (NIV).

Even without knowing how my lived experience with the Creator of heaven and earth would unfold, He assured me safe passage through the troubled waters and flames of adversity ignited by emotional and generational trauma:

> *"When you pass through the waters, I will be with you; and when you pass through the rivers, they will not sweep over you. When you walk through the fire, you will not be burned; the flames will not set you ablaze"*[5]

I emerged from my purposeful pause without pretending everything was okay, because I knew my lived experience with trauma was nothing but a chapter in the story of my life.

While you may not share my lived experience, your life is linked to an on-demand power source that you can access any time if you're willing to sit with what the soul wants to reveal. An intentional time out to reflect on unresolved issues might give birth to acts of resistance against disturbing or disruptive life events. It might also become an unexpected source of empowerment as the truth of your lived experience kicks in to help you put things in perspective—because "The most common way people give up their power is by thinking they don't have any."[6]

Our lived experience, whatever it might be, is but a chapter in the story of our lives because there's so much more to us than meets the eye.

Notes

— PART II —

The Quiet Work That Heals

Healing, recovery, and overcoming obstacles rarely occurs in the spotlight. Transformative life change unfolds during times of reflection — where we lay claim to the truth of who we are. It begins and ends with the willingness to sit with and consider our ways — with courage, empathy, and compassion.

CHAPTER 3

Mending Loose Ends

> *"Between every stimulus and response, there is a space. In that space is our power to choose. And in that choice lies our growth and our freedom."*
>
> — VIKTOR FRANKL

MY LONG WALK TOWARD FREEDOM from the shitty things that happened to me wasn't easy. At every step of the way, I had to decide, if I was going to resolve the issues posed by my lived experience or simply power my way through. I tried to power through, only to discover it's impossible to thrive and experience joy with unprocessed trauma riding shotgun in your life.

Over the years, I attempted to create a pathway uniquely my own through education and a public service career, but a few ratchet habits kept me in a holding pattern. Without knowing why, I stayed in relationships that drained my peace. I pursued emotionally unavailable partners. I sabotaged friendships to avoid commitment. I spent hours online rather than connecting with people in real time. I poured money into material comforts that never satisfied, resulting in bill-paying habits that created stress. Whenever a relationship didn't turn out as planned, my short-fused alter ego, *Hot Pockets,* would show up to turn the mutha out.

The deeper I dug my heels into powering through, the more disappointed I became. I couldn't explain the contradiction between what I had set my heart to, building a better life, and how I showed up. The mood swings experienced from one day to the next led to a continual stream of missed opportunities and fractured relationships I wish had turned out better.

For reasons that I could not name, I moved through life with a mind, body, and spirit that were not aligned. I considered myself successful, but I wrestled with feelings of insecurity, fear, and doubt. But as a life-long learner, I eventually came across an insight that revealed why building a better life presented such a challenge, "Trauma is the imprint of chronic, toxic stress on the mind and body, resulting in a feeling of powerlessness when we cannot overcome something or someone."[7]

The imprint of toxic stress is much more than a memory; it's the *unconscious searing* of behavior patterns on the mind, body, and spirit, which persists long after the events creating the impression have passed. The factors contributing to the imprint of toxic stress in my life included family separation, maternal grief and loss, and harmful sexual events tied to my younger years.

My continued search for answers to better understand myself led to the discovery of information about *emotional flatlining*. A trauma response disrupting the connection between mind, body, and spirit, making it difficult, if not impossible, to experience joy.

Emotional flatlining does its dirty work by attacking the emotional, social, and spiritual facets of health and wellness, resulting in a tendency to:

- Avoid social situations
- Pull away from romantic relationships and friendships
- Resist emotional and physical intimacy
- Entertain negative thoughts and feelings
- Mask true feelings and emotions [8]

I'm a living witness to how toxic stress and emotional flatlining can make it difficult to experience joy by making better choices.

The things I learned about myself marked the beginning of my foray into self-literacy. One of the most transformative interventions for restoring joy in my life turned out to be the *tough-love* questions I was willing to ask myself. The power of honest inquiry freed me from habits that escaped conscious awareness. The questions posed to better manage my coming-of-age story were simple but enlightening:

- What patterns of behavior am I repeating that are not helpful?
- What stories am I telling myself that perpetuate false narratives and unrealistic expectations?
- What opportunities am I avoiding because of insecurity or fear?

The answers to these questions empowered me to override patterns of behavior linked to toxic stress and emotional flatlining. Whenever I faced a difficult decision, a major transition, or a moment of doubt, I gave myself permission to pose tough-love questions to uncover what was tugging at my heartstrings. I never underestimated the power of epiphanies arising from tough love.

With the support of a mental health professional, I began to deal with the unprocessed trauma riding shotgun in my life—with courage and self-compassion. In the process, I acquired life skills to work through unresolved issues related to the loss of my family tree. I learned how to regulate my emotions and mend loose ends that made me look like a walking contradiction. I reclaimed my power to show up in ways that didn't betray my essence as a diamond in the rough. I latched on to the benefits offered by *self-awareness, emotional intelligence,* and *stress management practices* to rise above life's challenges. I finished what I started through our partnership by acknowledging that wholehearted living is possible even in the absence of support from immediate and extended family.

In time, I scaled the walls of resistance to intimacy, vulnerability, and connection by joining a support group for women. This was a diverse and lively sister circle that allowed me to dig up, dissect, and put some respect on the deepest parts of me. As we walked through the pages of *Healing for Damaged Emotions* [9], we engaged in real talk to acknowledge, release, and heal wounds that plagued us for years. Through the sacred work of mending loose ends, we reclaimed what our unresolved wounds tried to steal, our emotional freedom and joy. The lessons in living gained from the support group continue to shape my choices as a trauma-informed advocate of transformational life change.

Over the years I discovered the removal of toxic stress requires more than superficial changes. It's a lifelong call to action rooted in the soul's desire to return to its original shape and form, like memory foam. A few heart-centered practices that can aid in the removal process include:

- Journaling
- Mindfulness
- The creation of vision boards
- Time-outs and vacations for rest and relaxation
- Renewing the mind through inspirational writings
- Embracing the lighter side of life with levity, humor and comedy
- Movement of the body through exercise, dance, and other forms of creative expression

Each one of these practices can awaken and restore the connection between mind, body and spirit. What gets restored through the auspices of joy is not always visible. Sometimes it's the trust damaged by abandonment, betrayal, or neglect, the courage to begin again, or the ability to dream big.

Whenever I'm tempted to return to the habit of playing small, I glance at a plaque gifted to me by my daughter that reads, *"God is with you in all that you do,"* Genesis 21:22. I cling to this pithy reminder because the disruption of communication between mind, body, and spirit can occur at any time. The most common causes of disruption are:

- Indecision
- Procrastination
- Stagnation
- Ambivalence
- Lack of closure
- Unresolved personal and business matters

In times like these, we are not "broken" in need of fixing. Our inaction presents an opportunity to acknowledge the disconnect and find ways to restore communication between a transformative alignment that empowers us to:

- successfully manage the eight facets of health and wellness shaping our lives
- proactively monitor our emotional triggers and responses
- deepen our emotional intelligence

At its core, mending loose ends is about being proactive in resolving issues that hinder wholehearted living.

The Bible reminds us, "There is a time for everything, and a season for every activity under the heavens: a time to be born and a time to die, a time to plant and a time to uproot, a time to kill and a time to heal, and a time to tear down and a time to build."[10]. There's a lot to be said about these verses, but there's enough breathing room between the lines to include a time for mending loose ends, because we can heal whatever we allow ourselves to acknowledge and feel.

While empowerment, growth, and healing often occur in private—there are times when the wisdom and expertise of others, a *circle of care*, can help illuminate a path forward. A circle of care refers to the people who show up in your life to promote your well-being and growth across the emotional, physical, mental, and social facets of wellness.

This kind of collaboration reduces isolation, encourages vulnerability, and enables resource sharing. More than anything, it offers a safe space for talking about matters tugging at your heartstrings. Your circle of care might include a number of people, or yourself and one other person. While there is indeed strength in numbers, when it comes to a circle of care, the quality of support provided is far more important than numbers. If you're in need of a circle of care and wondering where to begin, here are some options you might want to consider:

- Family members and close friends who provide emotional support and understanding
- Mentors, coaches, or teachers who contribute to life skills development
- Colleagues who offer a reflective space for thoughtful conversations that help you process experiences, notice patterns, and make meaning of what's unfolding in your work life.
- You might choose to join a support group or community, in person or online, where you can speak freely, listen deeply, and learn about self-care practices that enhance self-literacy.
- You might consider working with a wellness coach who focuses on the whole person to help you set goals, cultivate self-aware-

ness, and integrate practical self-care tools across the eight facets of wellness.

- You might seek the support of a mental health professional—therapist, social worker, or counselor—who can help you process and work through trauma, grief, anxiety, and emotional wounds.
- You might find it helpful to connect with a peer support group or peer support specialist, where people with shared lived experiences walk alongside you—to offer encouragement and accountability tailored to your journey.

According to Dr. Bruce D. Perry, "Relationships are the agents of change, and the most powerful therapy is human love." A circle of care of your choosing can offer a safe space to do the quiet work that heals, build bridges of self-awareness, and deepen your own inner wisdom. As a diamond in the rough, you get to choose your cut.

Notes

CHAPTER 4

Resolving Inner Conflict

> *"Whenever you do something that is not aligned with the yearning of your soul, you create suffering."*
>
> — ANAÏS NIN

THE SEARCH FOR PATTERNS OF behavior that shaded my shine remained a work in progress for some time. With self-literacy, I began to see how the stories I told myself influenced the outcomes I experienced. Rather than slipping into the habit of casting myself in a negative light, I began reframing the stories I told myself. Instead of saying "I'm too sensitive," "I don't want to be a burden," or "I should be grateful to have a job," I flipped the script and said: "My sensitivity is a sign of emotional depth and awareness," "My talents are worthy of recognition and compensation," and "It's okay to ask others for help."

By reframing, I engaged my heart and mind in a process to bring about new ways of thinking. These *mini-affirmations* became a practical tool for chipping away at thought patterns that conceal the superpowers we all possess—*self-awareness* and *authenticity*.

Self-awareness as a life skill empowers us to understand ourselves from the inside out. In a broader sense, it involves recognizing how our thoughts, emotions, habits, strengths, challenges, and blind spots affect us and the people in our lives. Self-awareness is an act of resistance and empowerment.

According to Brené Brown, *authenticity* is the daily practice of letting go of who we think we're supposed to be and embracing who we are. Choosing authenticity means:

- Cultivating the courage to be imperfect, to set boundaries, and to allow ourselves to be vulnerable;
- Exercising the compassion that comes from knowing that we are all made of strength and struggle; and
- Nurturing the connections and sense of belonging that can only happen when we believe that we are enough.[12]

In looking back over my life, there were times when I was driven by ambivalence rather than these superpowers. As a normal part of the human experience, ambivalence shows up in feelings that pull us in different directions about an impending decision, issue, or person. On the surface, ambivalence is harmless. But when it lingers unresolved, it can trigger thought patterns, choices, and decisions that betray who we are.

My lived experience bears witness to what can happen when ambivalence becomes a driving force that causes us to forget who we are. The lapse that set me up for the ride of my life occurred during my public service career. For two decades, I contributed to the success of management and leadership teams. But workplace dynamics created barriers to stepping into more meaningful roles. The most challenging obstacle involved a three-year delay in receiving a hard-earned, well-deserved, and promised promotion.

The lack of movement by HR began to chip away at my confidence. The mental and emotional toll of waiting for the wheels of fairness and equity to turn resulted in feelings of frustration, anger, and resentment. I suffered in silence until my body refused to keep quiet.

I'll never forget the day paramedics rolled me out of City Hall on a stretcher to the nearest emergency room. After a series of tests, the attending physician told me I survived a hypertensive crisis that could have cost me my life.

During a brief leave of absence, I leaned into *reflective listening* to sit with what was true about my predicament. A familiar voice reminded me—"If one has courage, nothing can dim the light which shines from within."[13] In that moment, I had to face the fact that my ambivalence about advocating for myself and choosing to suffer in silence contributed to my demise.

After rolling through the valley of the shadow of death on a stretcher to ER, the battle lines had been drawn because—God did not give me a spirit of fear, but of power and of love and of a sound mind.[14]

At the end of my leave of absence, I pulled off the *flex* no one saw coming. I requested an audience with the gatekeeper of the city to plead my case. Within a week, the three-year impasse ended. I received a title change, a significant pay increase, and three years of retroactive pay.

I learned a few things about the importance of resolving inner conflict while going through this experience: "There comes a time when silence is betrayal," and "Behind the lines of opposition of any kind lies a pathway to freedom."

Even though I moved on from my employer with these lessons intact, I didn't always follow the path revealed by wisdom. My dating life became a mirror, reflecting the dilemma posed by loneliness, the fear of missing out, and ambivalence. While living single, I created a list of qualities desired in a mate:

- Someone who wasn't needy, competitive, possessive, or greedy.
- Someone with their own interests, hobbies, and career.
- Someone willing to support my life goals.
- Someone unafraid to speak the truth in love.
- Someone willing to work through rough patches without ghosting.
- Someone willing to set boundaries to support our coupling.
- Someone committed to becoming the best version of themselves.

My checklist was supposed to increase the odds of linking up with a person of integrity, but when I entered the dating scene, I didn't follow the desires of my heart. I allowed compromising stories to lead the way: "It's O.K. to lower your standards and have fun," "You'll be single forever with that checklist," and "Having a man is better than sitting home alone." It didn't take long for the fear of missing out to influence my decision-making. I ended up making my bed with a fella whose résumé included a stint behind prison walls.

The factors leading to my departure from self-awareness, authenticity, and my checklist were many. The absence of parents, extended family, and siblings to affirm my worth sent me looking for love in all the wrong places.

As a fatherless child, I didn't receive the wisdom a loving father might offer: "Don't rush into anything just to feel wanted," and "Never settle for a relationship that makes you forget who you are."

Without a BFF to run things by, I allowed wishful thinking and the thrill of companionship to gain the upper hand. Having a search and rescue mentality created another layer of vulnerability, which led to the creation of a startling chapter in my coming-of-age story.

My foray into uncharted territory, opened the door to outcomes I sought to avoid in any relationship: *being unseen, unheard, and misunderstood.*

> The transition from living my best life to a place where everything felt weighted was swift.
>
> I didn't have the chops to help a mate tethered to street smarts ascend to higher ground.
>
> Our alliance was fraught with mind-numbing shit I didn't know how to resolve.
>
> Disappointment surfaced whenever I reflected on the qualities desired in a mate.
>
> My self-confidence plummeted under the weight of fantasy and wishful thinking.
>
> The thrill of companionship simply disappeared.

I found myself living with the consequences of a decision that lacked discernment, a gift of the Spirit that speaks during soul-talking to keep us aligned with our hopes, dreams, and aspirations. Whenever we do something that is not aligned with the yearnings of our soul, we create suffering.

After revolving in a hot mess of my own making, I felt landlocked and imprisoned by sadness and anger. Letting go appeared to be the only option for experiencing better days. J. Martin Kohe said, "The greatest power that a person possesses is the power to choose." I released myself from the grip of sadness and anger by affirming, "The greatest power that I possess is the power to end and finish what I started."

I wrestled with my power to choose by coming up with reasons to remain landlocked rather than *pivot* and *shift*. As I cycled through feelings of embarrassment and shame, I landed on the deciding factor: What will people think? If being authentic meant letting go of who I thought I was supposed to be and embracing who I was, then my options were few. I decided to hightail it back to my checklist and get on with living the "Single Life."

There will be times when we will be challenged to go our own way, even if it means going it alone, for a time, a season, or an extended period of time.

As a diamond in the rough, I wasn't about to get cut, so I began plotting ways to tactfully end an uncharacteristic love story that never should have been written. As a woman who never embraced "Fake It Till You Make It" as a winning strategy, I exchanged the fear of missing out for "Fool Around and Find Out." In the days leading up to our uncoupling, I meditated on a three-word mantra, day and night, to mentally fast-track the process: "Separate to Elevate."

The courage to end and finish what I started arose from the stories I began to tell myself:

> "I'll meet the right person, but I need to end this shit as soon as possible."
>
> "There are many ways to fill the space created by loneliness."
>
> "I don't have to abandon my values to attract a partner."
>
> "God don't like ugly, and right about now I ain't looking so good."

The beliefs underlying these stories helped me to resolve issues posed by loneliness, the fear of missing out, and unresolved ambivalence.

In the days following our uncoupling, I found comfort in the wisdom of a woman in my circle of care with decades of marriage experience. Her counsel reminded me that choosing to end a mismatched relationship wasn't a failure—but a new beginning. A time to reclaim my voice and the power of choice. She affirmed that I didn't need to embark on a search and rescue mission to find a mate—my times were in the hands of the One who said, He would bless me with a future filled with hope—and success, not suffering."[15]

By aligning myself with a woman with the wisdom of years, the lived experience of marriage, and knowledge of the scriptures, I received counsel shaped by wisdom, faith, and love. These gifts of the Spirit allowed me to embrace my foray into uncharted territory as an unlikely source of empowerment, growth, and healing.

I've tapped into different supports over the years to make peace with the past because the quiet work that heals takes time. It's about creating space to flush out what really matters so better options can emerge. I spared myself many sleepless nights and avoided the high costs of settling for less by filtering my decision-making through an inquiry: *"Does the choice I'm about to make honor who I am, and who I am becoming?"* It's an inquiry that creates space to do the inner work and ground ourselves in choices that align with who we are and who we are becoming.

Notes

— PART III —

The Power of Wholehearted Living

With the free flow of information across social media, the internet, radio, podcasts, and television, we are never at a loss for information about what it means to live an authentic life. Yet there's something to be said about wholehearted living, which involves "building and living" a life from the ground up and inside out. This kind of living takes our truth to another level by chiseling our choices, refining our habits, and removing the shade from our shine.

Even though authenticity and wholehearted living are carved from the same rock, they're not the same because wholehearted living is a cut above authenticity. It requires grafting tools for living large on our hearts throughout our lifetime. In the process we become active participants in our ever-unfolding coming-of-age story.

As we open ourselves to empowering perspectives and practical tools that pave the way for whole-hearted living, we allow every facet of our health and wellness to grow, connect, and express itself.

CHAPTER 5

Seeking Higher Ground

"You wanna fly, you got to give up the shit that weighs you down."

— TONI MORRISON

THERE WERE TIMES WHILE SEEKING higher ground that I hit a wall because of the toxic baggage accumulated over the years. After many failed attempts, I learned how to fly by resolving an impairment that kept me grounded in shame. Brené Brown describes shame as "the intensely painful feeling or experience of believing you're flawed and unworthy of love and belonging."[16] For more years than I care to admit, shame covered me like a mist, creating a blind spot, which kept me from seeing myself as more than enough.

As an *instigator of doubt*, shame kept me from pursuing personal and business opportunities that appeared tailor-made for me. As a *perpetrator of comparison*, shame prompted me to idolize anyone blessed with a traditional family. My preoccupation was draining but never enough to stop the pity parties. Which often led to getting in where I fit in, even if it wasn't a good fit. As a *taskmaster*, shame offered unsolicited advice in mastering the art of perfection. Everything about me, the clothes I wore, how I styled my hair, and the car I drove, had to say, "I belong here."

Unfazed by my efforts to prove I was more than enough, shame kept me tethered to a mindset of limitation and lack, rather than freedom and possibility, in spite of my college education and public service career. One day I stumbled upon what turned out to be the cure for my visual impairment in the tenth chapter of the Book of Mark. Verses 46–52 provided a ringside seat to digest and reflect on a conversation between Jesus and a blind man seeking restoration of his sight.

The scene that drew me in occurred when Jesus told the man, "Go your way; your faith has made you well," and the man immediately regained his sight. Behind the scenes of what anyone could see, a heartbeat of faith emerged within the man's spirit, enabling him to regain his sight.

Reflecting on this passage reminded me that God has given each of us a measure of faith. It's not something we search for. It's already within us, ushering in breakthrough, healing, and relief when our hearts are ready to believe.[17]

I flipped the pages of my Bible to another passage that read, *"If you have faith as small as a mustard seed, you can say to this mountain, 'Move from here to there,' and it will move. Nothing will be impossible for you."*[18]

With these passages in mind, I started to believe I could move the weighted feelings birthed by shame that kept me grounded. I ended my time of reflection with the realization that the challenges posed by shame were not beyond the purview of Jesus or the measure of faith in me. Seeing myself in this light set me on a path to activating the healer within through *Inner Work.* I finally accepted the fact, after doing a *Reality Check,* that it's unwise to turn a blind eye to what was keeping me grounded.

Inner work involves delving into our thoughts, emotions, beliefs, and hidden behavior patterns—to better understand ourselves. The delving process can arise anytime, but more often than not, it comes whenever we feel we're holding on to something we need to release or when we sense something's got a hold of us. Inner work is the gift we give ourselves and the people we love by unearthing what makes us tick and what shuts us down.

I eased my way into inner work after acknowledging what resonated with me at the time. I don't believe there's a right or wrong way to begin because you know yourself better than anyone else. When and where you begin is up to you.

I decided to remove the emotional straitjacket I'd worn for years by replacing it with emotional freedom through *mindfulness*, *journaling*, and *self-reflection*. These heart-centered practices created space for the innermost parts of me, to see the light of day. Self-reflection and journaling led to the resurfacing of a handful of painful events I had to re-experience as a rite of passage.

To avoid being presumptuous about your familiarity with what I just shared, here's a brief description of each practice and why they are helpful in bridging the gap, no matter how small, between authenticity and wholehearted living.

> *Mindfulness involves paying attention to our thoughts, emotions, and surroundings—without judging them. It helps us notice what's happening on the inside before responding.*
>
> *Journaling involves writing down our thoughts and experiences to make sense of them. It's an activity that frees us to record anything of importance, express our emotions, monitor progress, and capture our hopes, dreams, and aspirations.*
>
> *Self-reflection involves looking inward to understand why we think, feel, and act the way we do. It invites honesty and insight, helping us connect our inner world with how we show up.*

These *Pathways to Becoming* work hand in hand to nurture empowerment, growth, and healing. Mindfulness teaches presence. Journaling gives our thoughts and emotions a landing place. And self-reflection allows us to connect with our innermost being. Together, they create space for seeking higher ground by helping us remove the things that weigh us down.

As I leaned in to these practices to get a better look at myself, several things emerged. While journaling, I found gifts and talents, shame did not want me to see. I never received training to be a life coach, mentor, or motivational speaker, yet the words etched in the pages of my journal said I was a natural when it came to encouraging and uplifting others.

Mindfulness and self-reflection revealed that my heart had not been hardened by the pains of life as shame wanted me to believe. Together, these Pathways of Becoming taught me that I was as free as I wanted to be in mind, body, and spirit. Without a home for sheltering in place, I kicked shame and all the shit that came with it to the curb.

The greatest gift received from inner work was the long-awaited release from the belief that I was damaged goods. Not from anything I did, but from the hand of cards life dealt, making me believe I was unworthy of love and belonging. This shift created space for grafting more tools for wholehearted living on my heart.

While putting everything I learned into play, I came across an empowering perspective that changed my life—which continues to illuminate my days and nights—the power of a growth mindset. This idea was shared with the world by Dr. Carol S. Dweck in *Mindset: The New Psychology of Success.*

The basic idea behind a growth mindset is this:

> When we believe that we can grow, learn, and improve, we tend to do just that. Our mind is a greenhouse capable of growing

whatever we plant and nurture with the right kind of care. We get to choose what gets planted—seeds of hope and perseverance or seeds of doubt and fear.

There is always potential for growth in the eight facets of wellness shaping our lives. We can cultivate an atmosphere for continued success by leaning into a growth mindset.

While there are many qualities associated with this idea, these are the heart postures that create a rhythm for making the transition from surviving to thriving a reality.

A Willingness to Learn by staying open to new ideas, skills, and constructive feedback, even when it feels uncomfortable.

Perseverance by leaning in and pressing forward, even when progress feels slow or difficult.

Resilience in bouncing back from mistakes, setbacks, and challenges without giving up.

Self-Compassion by extending understanding that mistakes are a natural part of the learning process, not a sign of failure.

Positive Self-Talk by choosing words that support growth.

Courage in stepping outside of our comfort zone to take on new challenges and risks.

Optimism in choosing to believe consistent effort pays off as an investment.

Patience in understanding that transformation takes time.

Perspective in giving yourself grace to view mistakes, delays, and disappointments as potential pathways for growth.

Humility in remaining open to constructive feedback by acknowledging there's always more to learn.

By leaning into these postures over the years, I removed the imprint of toxic stress, the inertia tied to emotional flatlining, and barriers to wholehearted living.

These mini-reflections highlight how pairing *heart postures* with *purposeful action* empowers us to stay the course while cultivating a growth mindset.

Believing I Could Do Hard Things

The hardest work I ever did came from turning inward to battle it out with shame. The battles weren't easy, and the wins weren't quick. But as I chiseled my way out of stories written by shame, something beautiful emerged—a deeper, wiser version of me.

Rocking Steady in the Face of Fear

There were moments when I almost gave up on the prospect of landing a good job or making new friends. But I reminded myself that courage was not the absence of fear and there are no dead ends. There were lessons embedded in every unexpected delay and disappointment. Positive self-talk and perseverance kept me from bailing out when all I heard was crickets after submitting a job application or texting someone I recently befriended. I discovered that staying the course in professional and personal life wasn't about maintaining control but about trusting the process—one day I'd reap what I had sown in the way of career readiness and relationship building.

Humbly Powering Through

There were times when I sought comfort in my journal, the keeper of secrets reflecting the deepest parts of me. Some entries were painful, while others radiated with glimmers of hope. But each one reminded me that growth is layered like the rings of a tree—bearing witness to time and season. Some entries bore witness to intense growth, while others spoke to drought and indecision. Self-compassion encouraged me to honor my worth as someone shaped by strength, struggle, joy, and pain. No matter the season, humility taught me how to remain fertile ground—by resisting the lure of bitterness. The entries penned on bended knee taught me the most—because my thoughts were prayers released into the atmosphere to irrigate the landscape of my life.

Throughout the years I discovered a growth mindset requires purposeful action because information alone does not produce transformation. These Action Steps might be helpful in bringing your hopes, dreams, and aspirations to life.

Step Into Yes
Growth begins when we decide to act. Being proactive is about taking ownership rather than waiting for circumstances to change. Each small step forward signals we're ready to trust the process.

Stay the Course
Having a plan provides direction and focus. When we define our goals, break them down into actionable steps, and monitor our progress, we can stay grounded when life becomes unpredictable.

Seek Genuine Connection
Growth blooms in the midst of laughter, rest, and mutually supportive relationships. Balancing productivity with play reminds us that joy and creativity are an important part of the growth process.

Seeking higher ground isn't about grinding or striving harder. It's about grounding ourselves in actions that expand our view of what's possible and moving in a way that frees us from anything that seeks to define rather than refine us.

Notes

CHAPTER 6

Growing With Grace

"Regardless of what you believe about spirituality, it's important to bring a sense of the sacred into your everyday life."

— DR. CHRISTIANE NORTHRUP

WE EACH HAVE OUR OWN way of bringing the sacred into everyday life. For some, spirituality is expressed through prayer; for others, it shows up in worship, creativity, time in nature, journaling, acts of service, or times of reflection. Our spirituality and what we believe lives in the choices we make, the compassion we extend, and the gratitude we carry.

By inviting the sacred into our lives, we can elevate ordinary moments into precious memories. A daily gratitude practice that begins with "What am I grateful for today?" can be helpful in acknowledging what we're thankful for.

Over the years, I learned that a grateful heart can smooth the jagged edges of life and straighten the crooked paths I've stumbled upon along the way. The things I'm grateful for and honor each day are the gift of life, breath in my lungs, a sound mind, a Good Shepherd watching over me, and a heart surrendered to the wisdom of the Serenity Prayer:

> *"God, grant me the serenity to accept the things I cannot change, courage to change the things I can, and wisdom to know the difference."*
>
> —*Reinhold Niebuhr*

Living with a heart surrendered to the wisdom of this prayer mattered most when I'd done my best to build a better life, but found myself at a crossroads, unsure of my next steps. On those days, grace appeared in one way or another to move me one step closer to what seemed out of reach—living a life of significance without the covering of a family tree. Grace gave me the courage to honor the fact that some things never change, but get better when released by faith to the redemptive work of grace.

Many, if not all, of the things we enjoy in life are manifestations of grace: uncommon favor and blessings. Grace is not a backup plan when all else fails, a lucky charm, or an appendage to free will. Grace is a life force and energy, a source of inspiration for tired and weary souls, sitting at the crossroads of life.

The touch and feel of grace is revealed by what it empowers us to do and become. It never dictates or commands—but gently invites us to decide what's next in our quest to cultivate a growth mindset. Grace empowers us to persevere when everything seems off-kilter. Grace doesn't make a grand entrance but subtly appears when we least expect it in parenting, recovery, relationship building, and everything in between.

Grace in Parenting:

There were days when I ran out of patience as a single mother, responding with irritation when all my children needed was tenderness and unconditional love. And yet—grace made room for me to circle back, even when I felt depleted, to show up with what my children and I needed.

What I needed most in the early days of parenting was the fruit of the Spirit—love, joy, peace, patience, kindness, goodness, faithfulness, gentleness, and self-control. These are ways of being that simplify what I often found myself complicating. Over the years I became a better parent by calibrating my steps to the rhythms of grace that invaded my space during times of exhaustion and burn-out.

Grace in Recovery:
I've battled through trauma, failed relationships, and self-sabotage. The path to healing hasn't been easy—it's been messy, uneven, and imperfect. But I'm still here, sustained by nothing but grace.

Grace in Relationships:
There were moments when a sharp word or misunderstanding could have fractured a friendship. Instead, grace entered in through my friend's willingness to "Seek first to understand, then to be understood", leaving the door open for continued connection.

These moments of lift and elevation allowed me to see that grace meets us where we are.

While my own encounters of growing with grace have shaped my life, I've witnessed its reach beyond my lived experience. The following reflections are a gift of the heart, offered to encourage readers drawn to this book. The first comes from a woman on the rise who entered my life through a friendship with my daughter, and the other from a sister by heart not blood, to reveal how grace visits every generation.

> ***Grace Is in the Eyes of the Beholder***
> *Grace, to me, is the quiet strength that shows up when life hands you moments you never believed you could survive. It's not loud, and it doesn't always feel comforting at first. But it shows itself in the spaces between heartbreak and growth—in*

the places where you learn you're still standing, even when you thought you couldn't.

I first learned the true meaning of grace when I experienced the loss of my infant daughter. There are no words that prepare you for that kind of pain. In that moment, grace wasn't about feeling strong—it was about being held together by something greater than my own understanding. It was the breath that reminded me to keep going, the whisper that told me that my story didn't end in that moment of loss. Grace carried me through the darkest emptiness and slowly taught me how to live with both love and grief at the same time.

Grace appeared again years later in a completely different way—through my relationship with my mother. Growing up without her around much wasn't easy, and the distance between us shaped a lot of who I became. But then life shifted: she had a devastating stroke, and suddenly I was the one caring for her day and night.

In a way I never expected, life brought me back to a place of nurturing—a role I longed to have with my own child but never got the chance to fulfill. Now, caring for my mother as she moves through a vulnerable, almost infant-like stage after her stroke has become a tender reminder that grace sometimes returns what was taken, but in a form we didn't imagine. It doesn't replace the loss, but it shows me that the ability to nurture, love, and protect still lives in me.

Becoming her caregiver forced me to confront old wounds, but even more, it invited me into a space of compassion I didn't know I had. Grace showed me that healing doesn't always come from apologies—sometimes it comes from responsibility, patience, and showing up for someone who couldn't show up for you.

Grace softened my heart in ways I never expected. It helped me see my mother not just through the lens of the past, but as a human being who needed love, understanding, and forgiveness.

Through loss, through rebuilding, through caregiving, grace has become the guide that helps me navigate challenges I once thought would break me. It reminds me that strength isn't always loud. Sometimes it's the simple choice to keep loving, to keep trying, and to keep opening your heart even after it's been hurt.

Grace, to me, is the unseen hand that lifts you when life tries to pull you under—the force that helps you grow through pain, rise through responsibility, and find purpose in moments that once felt impossible.

The following reflection reveals how grace empowered my sister to resolve inner conflict and the fear of decision-making that comes with adulting, while trusting grace to meet her daily and future needs.

Growing with Grace in Decision-Making

Life decisions can be complicated, yet they become part of our journey as we learn to make choices for ourselves. Since we are born with our own DNA blueprint, it makes us different and unique. In my own experience, my parents made decisions for me until I was old enough to make them for myself.

During my childhood and teenage years, I was never challenged on my decision-making by anyone with the exception of my parents. As I grew into adulthood, I found making decisions to be overwhelming, unsure if I was making the right choice based on my dignity and worth. I was totally afraid of criticism from others because it made me feel uncomfortable, at a lower standard, and incapable of making sound decisions.

But as life went on, I had to evaluate my fear of allowing myself to make my own decisions without letting others critique them. Not all criticism is bad. Some critics have good points and information you can use to weigh the pros and cons before making a major decision. For example, I have heard many people, including myself, say 'If only I had considered this' or 'I should have followed my first mind,' as if the decision would change. For me I think this is an extra burden that weighs on our lives because you can't change the outcome of something that has already been decided, which can leave you feeling disappointed with yourself or the results.

My parting thought about decision-making is this: Make the best decision you can, without doubting yourself because what is meant for you is for you. What isn't meant for you simply means something greater is waiting. Whatever situation you face, remember it is your decision to make.

Together, these reflections reveal what it means to be *Chiseled by Choices*. They also convey with transparency and uniqueness that grace does more than comfort; it empowers us to thrive in an ever-changing world by transforming how we navigate life's challenges.

No matter the season, we are never alone, because there's always more to us than meets the eye, with grace by our side. The enabling power of grace becomes a chisel in the hand of the one willing to make courageous choices.

Most of us can agree that when it comes to growth, change, and transition, it takes courage to acknowledge how our daily decisions shape what we experience in life. *Growing with Grace* is an empowering perspective, a lifelong invitation, and an enduring call—to bring the sacred into our daily lives.

By drawing on the gifts of the Spirit we all possess—*curiosity and imagination*—we can regulate how we respond to life's challenges by showing up in a way that allows grace to appear in our time of need. As we leverage these gifts of the spirit, we become architects of our own transformation.

The daily routines I created to help me respond to life's challenges in a way that contributed to my own empowerment, growth, and healing included a *Reality Check*, a *Pivot and Shift* maneuver, and a *Power Up*—fueled by small, intentional actions.

These routines allowed me to conserve precious energy, avoid shading my shine, and simplify what I had a tendency to complicate. After leaning into these routines over the years, they began to surface, like an on-demand pop-up shop, to provide what I needed when I found myself embroiled in a heated conversation or an emotionally charged disagreement with a family member, colleague, or friend.

I'm sharing the essence of these routines, hoping they offer support in making the most of your days and nights, by creating space for reflection, rebooting, and purposeful action.

Reality Check

At the heart of a reality check is this: "You better check yourself before you wreck yourself." It's an honest, compassionate look at what is actually happening—inside of you, and with the people, places, and situations that present a challenge—without denial, drama, or blaming others for feelings that are actually coming from inside of you. It means identifying what is true about the situation you are facing, and responding with honesty and courage rather than reinventing what's happening through words and actions that misrepresent and mischaracterize the truth of the matter.

Pivot and Shift

This routine allows you to get out of harm's way arising from friendly fire that originates from your own thoughts, the creation of unrealistic expectations, or self-sabotage. When you pivot and shift, you give yourself an opportunity to choose a new way of thinking and responding whenever you find yourself drifting into old ways and patterns of behavior that have not been helpful. Especially if you've grown used to being in a holding pattern or stuck in a rut—or made living with unresolved issues your constant companion. It takes self-discipline to pivot and shift and admit "this is how I've always responded," but "this is how I choose to respond in the here and now."

This routine also works to re-position yourself for success when you find yourself in an unhealthy relationship or situation that ignores your values or compromises your worth. Pivoting and shifting can look like setting new relationship or workplace boundaries, limiting the amount of time spent with or invested in certain people, or choosing to opt out altogether.

Power Up

A power up is an intentional choice made after cycling through a reality check that invites you to pivot and shift. It's a concrete step and purposeful action taken to exercise agency, choice, and free will in resolving one or more issues that haven't seen the light of day in years. A power up is not about control; it's about aligning your actions and choices with your values and what matters most.

The small intentional acts that can fuel a power up are endless. A few ideas worth considering include:

- Repeating an affirmation.
- Reviewing a Note to Self, strategically placed at home or work, with an uplifting reminder to help you ascend to higher ground.
- Listening to a favorite song or playlist.

- Connecting with someone in your circle of care to vent and decompress.
- Drawing on the memory of overcoming another challenge to affirm, "I've got this!."
- Reflecting on a Bible verse or passage to crossover from where you are to where you want to be.

These routines and many others have a way of exposing old habits that no longer serve us. Each one proves that we are not powerless to change. From a wellness perspective, these routines make us active participants in restoring balance and synergy to our mind, body, and spirit and the various facets of our health and wellness. Together, they become the gift we give ourselves to experience the best life has to offer.

I'm not a spiritual guide, but I'd be remiss if I didn't share what a search for "the benefits of bringing the sacred into everyday life" revealed:

> *Bringing spirituality and the sacred into everyday life offers profound benefits, including reduced stress, greater purpose, improved mental and physical health, stronger relationships, enhanced resilience, a deeper sense of joy and peace, a sense of connection to something larger than yourself, and the ability to transform mundane tasks into meaningful experiences.*

If you're interested in taking a deeper dive to explore these benefits, you can use my search terms or create your own.

As of late, I've been drawn to the idea that "less is more," so my thoughts on the benefits of living this kind of life are simple. Our days become brighter, our mind finds comfort in simplicity and clarity, our heart is strengthened by what each day offers, and our spirit remains receptive to the visitations of grace. Our nights become an oasis for experiencing positive life change through whatever brings us joy, such as:

- Family time.
- Meal time.
- Dinner dates.
- Movie nights.
- Creative endeavors.
- Mixing playlists and music tracks.
- Exercise.
- Caregiving.
- Meditation.
- Walking in nature.
- Journaling.
- Reading an inspiring book.
- Quiet moments of reflection.

There are many other activities that could be added to this list, which is simply a sampling of what might draw our attention. Growing in grace is a way of life that transforms our days and nights. Through small, intentional acts, done consistently, we become guardians of what we need most to make the transition from surviving to thriving in everyday life.

Epilogue: Chiseled by Choices, Crowned by Courage

"Everyone has a divine purpose for being on the planet."

– DR. HADIYAH-NICOLE GREEN

Before parting ways, I'd like to share a few thoughts about divine purpose and calling, because everyone has one. It's not something we create—but something we embrace as a part of our coming-of-age story. It's an assignment that aligns with our gifts, talents, and lived experience. When unburdened by fear, anxiety, and doubt, our divine purpose and calling anchor us in a power far greater than ourselves.

The call that beckons us to respond to divine purpose can occur at any time:

- *In adolescence*, it may emerge as the courage to be seen and heard without shrinking—to speak truth and take up space as a poet, songwriter, or advocate for those without a voice.
- *In young adulthood*, it may unfold as a call to create, lead, or chart a path as a charismatic team leader, mentor, or ambassador of a social cause focused on one of the big "pillars" that hold up community life—like education, health, the environment, economic opportunity, human rights, and community safety.

- *In our thirties*, it may lead to opportunities where our voice, vision, and vitality are needed to support positive life change, as a life coach, counselor, or therapist.
- *In our forties,* it may beckon us to become a nonprofit leader, artist, or spiritual guide.
- *In our fifties*, it may reveal itself in the freedom to tell our story as an author, advocate for justice, or champion of wellness.
- *In our sixties, and beyond*, it may unfold with a request to become a gentle navigator and guide to women on the rise.

These are simply examples of the way people may be called, in different seasons of life, to live out their divine purpose. The possibilities are endless.

Our calling, whatever it may be, will never cease to exist because we can't outrun or escape its reach. Through trial and error and serendipity, we transcend the stories, fears, and beliefs that try to keep us from succeeding. But in time, we emerge victorious with our mind, body, and spirit intact—ready, willing, and able to embrace our reason for being here.

"The journey of a thousand miles begins with a single step."
—Lao Tzu

No matter the struggles encountered along the way, it's never too late to align with our divine purpose and calling. There will be times when it feels like we are carrying weights that impede our progress. That's when we need to pause and turn on the searchlight of our hearts to see what's standing in our way. In this book, courage has been revealed as a way of moving through life—by making life-affirming choices, even when they are unpopular among people we're linked to by birth, chance, or choice.

The path leading to my calling to become an author wasn't neat, tidy, or linear—but it's always been heart-centered, intentional, and honest. When I finally stopped waiting for acceptance and permission from the powers that be in the book publishing industry to share my work, I found the courage to pursue my passion and Flyte Time Publications was born.

Volume I of the Life Change Series, *It's Time to Turn Up, No More Trauma*, celebrates the power of owning our stories and making peace with the past. The calls-to-action woven throughout the text affirm what I know is true—buried beneath the surface of every coming-of-age story lies an inner strength and body of truth capable of changing the trajectory of our lives.

Each chapter in Volume II, *Chiseled by Choices, Reflections on Empowerment, Growth and Healing*, extends an invitation to engage in the most important work of your life, because when you allow the transformative power of pain to have her perfect work, you uncover valuable lessons hidden from view.

As you draw from the well of lived experience, you learn to trust your inner wisdom and voice. When you pick up the pieces and mend loose ends, you put an end to the depletion of your personal power. As you resolve inner conflict, you free yourself to live your best life. When you seek higher ground, you transcend things that try to weigh you down. As you embrace grace for change, you open your heart to a life force and energy that never disappoints.

Without knowing what prompted you to buy this book, I'm standing in agreement with your desire to invest in yourself to experience breakthrough and liberation from whatever stands between you and the fulfillment of your divine purpose. Whether you're navigating a season of change, grappling with indecision, or making peace with some aspect of your past, I hope the information shared in this volume builds bridges of understanding to help you realize your hopes, dreams, and aspirations.

As a diamond in the rough, you get to choose your cut and transform your coming-of-age story into a thing of beauty by revealing what a woman on the rise looks like.

May your inner light continue to burn bright—to reveal the path forward into the best days of your life.

Thank you for choosing this moment, this work, this journey.

With deep love and honor,

Lady D

Notes

1. Dr. Peggy Swarbrick, *Wellness in 8 Dimensions Guide: Exploring Strengths and Building New Wellness Habits* (Free PDF, Collaborative Support Programs of New Jersey, 2025), https://cspnj.org/wellness-institute/.
2. "Expressive Therapies," *Wikipedia*, last modified August 29, 2025, https://en.wikipedia.org/wiki/Expressive_therapies.
3. Maya Angelou, *Rainbow in the Clouds: The Wisdom and Spirit of Maya Angelou* (New York: Random House, 2014).
4. Marianne Williamson, *A Return to Love: Reflections on the Principles of A Course in Miracles* (New York: HarperCollins, 1992).
5. *Isaiah* 43:2, New International Version (NIV).
6. Alice Walker, *Possessing the Secret of Joy* (New York: Harcourt Brace Jovanovich, 1992).
7. Natalie Y. Gutiérrez, *The Pain We Carry: Healing from Complex PTSD for People of Color* (Oakland: New Harbinger Publications, 2022).
8. Tree House Recovery, "What Is Anhedonia and What Causes It?" paraphrased and adapted.
9. David A. Seamands, *Healing for Damaged Emotions* (Wheaton, IL: David C. Cook, 1981).
10. Ecclesiastes 3:1–3 , New International Version (NIV).
11. Unknown
12. Brené Brown, *The Gifts of Imperfection: 10th Anniversary Edition* (New York: Random House, 2020), 68.
13. Maya Angelou, *Letter to My Daughter* (New York: Random House, 2008).
14. *2 Timothy* 1:7, New King James Version (NKJV).
15. *Jeremiah* 29:11, Contemporary English Version (CEV).
16. Brené Brown, "Shame vs. Guilt," *Brené Brown Blog*, January 15, 2013, https://brenebrown.com/articles/2013/01/15/shame-v-guilt/.
17. Romans 12:3, New International Version (NIV).
18. Matthew 17:20, New International Version (NIV).

Figure 1 Tree of Wellness

Lady D's Playlist

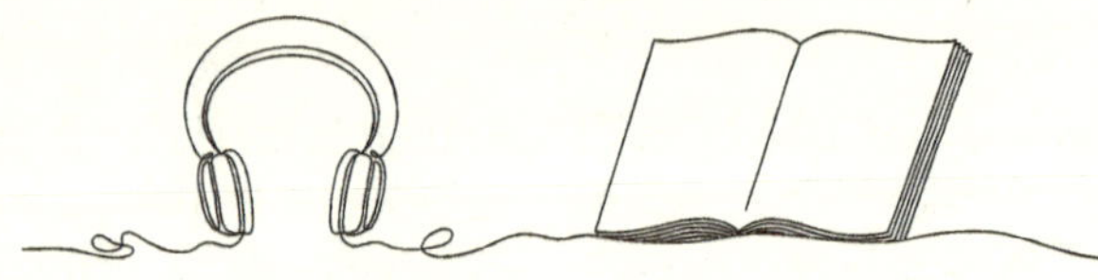

Music Is My Way of Life—Patti Labelle

Stand—Sly & The Family Stone

Don't Worry, Be Happy—Bobby McFerrin

Exodus—Bob Marley & The Wailers

Home—Stephanie Mills

Optimistic—Sounds of Blackness

We Gon' Be Alright—Tye Tribbett

Angel—Angela Winbush

About the Author

Lady D is a certified peer support specialist and trauma-informed advocate of transformational life change. She is a foster-care system alumna, unapologetic encourager, and proponent of wholehearted living. Throughout her multi-faceted career, she has served women, young adults, and at-risk teens by sharing heart-centered guidance and uncommon wisdom to support them in overcoming obstacles posed by their coming-of-age story. Her commitment to advocacy and empowerment through self-determination arose while earning a bachelor's degree in criminal justice and a Juris Doctorate in Law.

Having served on executive, leadership, and management teams in the public and private sector for over three decades, she currently spends her time uplifting the lives of contemporaries, millennials, elders, and the next generation by any means necessary.

About Flyte Time Publications

Flyte Time Publications stands as a beacon of light and conveyor of hope in the midst of hard times. The *Life Change Series* elevates readers by demystifying the pathways available to heal emotional wounds related to traumatic and disruptive life events. The series amplifies stories rooted in lived experience to honor and acknowledge accessibility to the gifts of the spirit every reader can use to successfully navigate the human experience and fulfill their potential. Each work empowers readers through truth-telling, self-discovery, and soul-stirring calls-to-action.

Website: www.flytetimepublications.com
Email: LadyD@flytetimepublications.com
Phone: (424) 312-6347

Here are a few ways you can support me and my work.

Your Words Have Power

If you've made it to the end of this book, thank you for spending this time with me. My hope is that somewhere along the way, you felt seen, heard, and understood.

Books like this travel—from one home to the next, because someone was willing to say, "I think you'd like this book."

One of the most meaningful ways you can help is by sharing a few words about your experience.

Would you consider leaving a brief book review?

Even a sentence or two—a few choice words about what stood out—can help someone else decide if this book is worth their time and investment.

Scan to leave your review—it only takes a moment.

Thank you for using your voice!

Continuing the Conversation

If something within these pages challenged you, comforted you, or met you where you are and sparked a desire to take a deeper dive through continued conversation, I'd love to hear from you. I review and respond to every message received.

You can message me at **LadyD@flytetimepublications.com**, using the subject line "*Chiseled by Choices.*" I'm a resourceful, resilient, and unselfish Peer Support Advocate with lived experience and gratuitous wisdom to share.

Sharing Your Story

The next book in the Life Change series will focus on *living in the overflow of light, love, and legacy.* Volume 3 will include personal stories from contributors who share how self-advocacy and self-determination have influenced how they see themselves, their relationships, their future, and the legacy they're creating by living out loud.

If that sounds like you, and you're interested in shaping the narrative of a book focused on passing on what matters most to the next generation, you can send a 500 to 750 word original, personal story by email to **LadyD@flytetimepublications.com** using the subject line "Volume 3 Inquiry."

Every submission will be acknowledged, and the content of your story—as well as the selection process—will be kept confidential. Stories included in the book will not use contributors' full names or identifying details. Publication of any selected story will be by mutual agreement.

As a thank you, all contributors who submit a story—whether it is selected for inclusion or not—will receive a complimentary copy of Volume 3 upon publication in early 2027.

Chiseled by Choices:

A Personal Wellness Workbook

Tough-Love Questions for Living with Intention Across the Eight Facets of Wellness

How to Use This Workbook

This workbook was created to be used slowly, honestly, and without performance. It is not a test. It is not a checklist. It is an invitation to pause, reflect, and make intentional choices.

You may work through the facets in order or begin with the area that feels most urgent. There is no right pace. Growth does not require speed—it requires truth.

Each facet includes:

- A brief reflection to ground the topic
- Tough-love questions to prompt self-inquiry
- Space for notes, journaling, or commitments

Return to these pages as often as needed. What matters is not completing the workbook, but engaging with it.

The Tree of Wellness

The Tree of Wellness depicts eight interconnected facets of well-being that shape our lives.

Like branches on a tree, each facet subtly influences how we grow and flourish in the others.

This workbook invites you to reflect on each facet with curiosity and honesty so that every facet can grow, connect, and express itself.

FACET ONE:
Emotional Wellness

Reflection

Emotional wellness asks us to be honest about what we feel and courageous enough to respond rather than react. Avoided emotions do not disappear—they resurface through our choices.

Tough-Love Questions

What emotions do I routinely suppress because acknowledging them feels inconvenient or unsafe?

In what situations do I minimize my feelings to keep the peace?

When was the last time I allowed myself to fully feel disappointment without rushing to fix it?

How do my unprocessed emotions show up in my relationships or decisions?

What emotion is asking for my attention right now?

Choice + Action

One emotional boundary I need to set is:

One feeling I will honor without judgment this week is:

FACET TWO:

Environmental Wellness

Reflection

Our environments influence our clarity, energy, and sense of safety. Disorder outside often mirrors overwhelm within.

Tough-Love Questions

What in my environment consistently drains my energy?

Which spaces feel restorative, and why?

Where have I normalized chaos because change feels like too much work?

What physical space reflects how I truly want to live?

Choice + Action

One small environmental change I can make now is:

One boundary I need to create around my space is:

FACET THREE:

Financial Wellness

Reflection

Financial wellness is not about wealth—it is about dignity, agency, and peace of mind. Our money choices often reveal our fears and values.

Tough-Love Questions

What money story am I still living out?

Where do I avoid looking at my finances because it triggers anxiety or shame?

How does my spending align—or conflict—with what matters most to me?

What financial habit would most improve my sense of freedom?

Choice + Action

One financial behavior I am willing to change is:

One step toward financial clarity I will take is:

FACET FOUR:

Intellectual Wellness

Reflection

Intellectual wellness keeps us curious and open. Growth stalls when we stop questioning what we think we already know.

Tough-Love Questions

When was the last time I challenged a belief I've held for years?

What topics do I avoid because they disrupt my comfort?

How do I continue learning outside of obligation?

In what ways do I underestimate my capacity to grow intellectually?

Choice + Action

One topic I want to explore more deeply is:

One habit that supports my mental growth is:

FACET FIVE:

Occupational Wellness

Reflection

Occupational wellness is about meaning, not titles. It asks whether how we spend our time aligns with who we are becoming.

Tough-Love Questions

Does my daily work reflect my values or simply my survival?

Where do I feel unseen or undervalued?

What part of my work drains me the most—and why?

How might I redefine success on my own terms?

Choice + Action

One adjustment I can make to align my work with purpose is:

One boundary I need to set around my time is:

FACET SIX:

Physical Wellness

Reflection

The body remembers what the mind forgets. Physical wellness requires attention, not perfection.

Tough-Love Questions

How do I treat my body when I am stressed?

Where have I ignored signals that something needs care?

What routines support my strength and energy?

How does rest factor into my definition of productivity?

Choice + Action

One physical habit I will prioritize is:

One signal from my body I will respect is:

FACET SEVEN:

Social Wellness

Reflection

Connection shapes our sense of belonging. The quality of our relationships often mirrors the quality of our boundaries.

Tough-Love Questions

Who truly supports my growth?

Where do I over-give to feel valued?

Which relationships require honest conversations?

How do I show up when connection feels uncomfortable?

Choice + Action

One relationship I want to nurture differently is:

One boundary I need to reinforce is:

FACET EIGHT:

Spiritual Wellness

Reflection

Spiritual wellness grounds us in meaning beyond circumstance. It is the anchor that holds when everything else shifts.

Tough-Love Questions

What gives my life meaning beyond achievement?

How do I reconnect with purpose during uncertainty?

Where do I resist stillness?

What practices help me feel aligned and centered?

Choice + Action

One spiritual practice I will return to is:

One intention I will carry forward is:

INTEGRATION:

Living Chiseled by Choices

Closing Reflection

- Growth requires discernment.
- Discernment requires honesty.
- Honesty requires courage.

Use the insights gained from these pages to make choices that reflect who you are becoming—not who you have been.

www.ingramcontent.com/pod-product-compliance
Lightning Source LLC
LaVergne TN
LVHW090611110826
845146LV00001B/349

* 9 7 9 8 9 8 7 1 7 8 9 4 2 *